YOU
CAN'T
BULLY
ME

A GUIDE FOR KIDS
TO WIN CONFIDENCE
AND LOSE A BULLY

LINDA LANDES

BALBOA
PRESS
A DIVISION OF HAY HOUSE

I am not a psychologist, therapist, social worker or counselor. This book
comes from my personal experiences, and situations that occurred with
students during my years as a teacher of elementary school children.

Balboa Press books may be ordered through booksellers or by contacting:

Balboa Press
A Division of Hay House
1663 Liberty Drive
Bloomington, IN 47403
www.balboapress.com
1 (877) 407-4847

Print information available on the last page.

ISBN: 978-1-5043-2623-0 (sc)
ISBN: 978-1-5043-2624-7 (hc)
ISBN: 978-1-5043-2625-4 (e)

Library of Congress Control Number: 2015902607

Balboa Press rev. date: 3/30/2015

Contents

The mosaic design on your writing
pages is for you to color.
Do not use markers.
You are creating something unique, and
realizing while you work that
you
are
unique.

Introduction For Kids

You Can't Bully Me was written about you and for you. With the help of this book, you will make friends with yourself, accept who you are, and live a happier life.

My goal is to help you become more confident. Not so simple all the time, but look around at the kids in your class who aren't bullied. There's something about them and how they feel about themselves that discourages the bully. What do you think?

I promise that you will feel better before you get to the last page. If there are difficult vocabulary words, please take some time to sit with someone who can talk with you about what the words really mean and how you can grow into them.

In "The Wizard of Oz," Dorothy and her friends go in search of the Wizard because they believe he will give them brains, a heart, courage and a way home. By the time they escape the Wicked Witch and go back to the

Wizard with the broom, the Wizard points out that they already possessed these attributes, only they didn't realize it. In Dorothy's case, the Good Witch tells her that she had the power all along but had to find it out on her own. This is what we are going to do: you have the brains, heart, courage and power to make your way; you just need to believe it and believe in yourself.

Here's the thing......bullying happens to everyone. How you react to it when it happens is another thing, and for many of us, the most difficult thing. There are lessons to be learned from the experience, for example what friendship is, that make it an important topic to study. Sadly, this will not be the only time in your life when bullying happens, but it will be the last time it hurts in the way you're hurting now.

Which of these statements is true for you?
I am so embarrassed.
I deserve to be bullied.
I feel ashamed of myself.
The bully is right about me.
I am not special.
I can't be special if someone is trying to hurt me.

In many of the movies you know, the main character has a problem of some kind. The songs that become famous are all pep talks: let it go, be brave, sing when you are afraid, you can do it.

When things are hard for you, you absolutely must find a way to remember that things will get better and work towards that goal.

Who taught you how to walk? You taught yourself. Something across the room got your interest and as soon as you were aware that you could move your body to get to it, off you went. Do you remember all the times you fell down? Of course not. You didn't understand language yet, so no one could teach you. This book will 'teach' you in the same way – reminding you what you already know about how great you are.

Bullying Story: When I was teaching fifth grade, a student in my class bullied some second grade girls every day at lunch by calling them ugly and stupid. They did the right thing by reporting it to their teacher, who told me about it. I called the girls into my classroom to write down their names; I wanted my student to write apology letters to each of them. Something made me ask them if they believed what the girl had said. Two said no, but two said yes. I asked them why they would believe the words of a mean girl. They didn't know.

This book is for them and for you. How can the words of a mean person be more important than your own feelings about yourself? The bully doesn't know you. The bully doesn't care about you. You have to believe so much in yourself and the kind of person you are that no one's words can hurt you. You Can't Bully Me will help you learn about the most important person in your life – you!

When life knocks you down, roll over and look at the stars.

The bully in your life is probably making you feel miserable. We're going to change that. By the time we are done, you will feel so good about yourself, I think the bully will get bored with you and will leave you alone. I believe that confidence and really knowing who you are will make you more interesting to the right people and the words of a bully won't mean anything to you. The bully is not, nor will ever be, your friend. Let me say this again: The bully is not, nor will ever be, your friend. We will discuss this more a little later.

You don't need anyone's permission to feel good and love yourself.

If you make friends with yourself, you will never be alone. It is really hard to be by yourself, but sometimes it is the best place to be. Being alone gives you time to focus on your hobbies, listen to the music you like, read about things that interest you, help out family or neighbors, and learn things you don't learn about in school.

The activities that follow are to be done one day at a time, but always one day after the other; please don't try to race through. I would like you to think about each topic and write what is in your heart; there are no wrong answers. If you feel more comfortable, you can write on notebook paper. Simply write the page number and title on the top so you can keep track.

The first thing that comes into your mind as you answer each question is your truth. It is what you believe with all your heart. You are writing for yourself, and no one else. There are no wrong answers. These opinions and feelings will most likely be the things that you can't be bullied about. Find strength and comfort in your own words.

Oh, yeah, and color the design on your writing pages. After all, this is your book. I also want you to write a compliment to yourself in color on the top of each page so that when you thumb through the book, you have a reminder of who you are. I think you will like what you read.

Highlight or underline sentences you like so you can read them again as you go along.

Activity: Complete this sentence: People tell me I am special because.......

_____

_____

_____

_____

_____

_____

_____

_____

Activity: Complete this sentence: I know I am special because......

_____

_____

_____

_____

_____

_____

_____

_____

_____

_____

_____

_____

_____

_____

_____

_____

_____

_____

_____

_____

_____

You are special all the time. You are special when you are good and you are special when you are not so good. Your personality, your sense of humor and your view of the world all make you special and unique. Remember that when you feel sad.

You're spending a lot of time worrying about what other people think. Their opinions don't matter. Any time you think you are "too" anything, you are trying to change for someone. I cry when I watch movies. People tell me

I am too sensitive. Maybe I am. But, maybe they are not sensitive enough.

There is an old story that goes something like this:

An old man told his grandchild, "There is a battle between two wolves inside all of us. One is Evil. It is anger, jealousy, greed, resentment, inferiority, lies and ego.

The other is Good. It is joy, peace, love, hope, kindness, humility, empathy and truth."

The child thought about it and asked, "Grandfather, which wolf wins?"

The old man quietly replied, "The one you feed."

Do you understand this? The bully is mean, and yes, I think you can even say evil. If, indeed, bad and good live inside us all, and you pay attention and try being Good, your life will be easier and feel happier.

The same advice applies for honesty. Do you know it's very hard work to tell a lie? You have to remember exactly what you said forever, and who you said it to because if you ever mess up, you'll get caught and hurt a relationship with someone.

So, don't lie to yourself either. Be honest when you do your writing. You know how you feel. If you don't know how to answer a question, think about it for a day or two before you write. You can always change your mind, you know.

The cover design is a mosaic because each tile is needed to make the picture. The mosaic that is you is made of little 'tiles' that are your personality and character. At the same time, you are a tile in a larger mosaic, the one that makes up the world. So very special and important.

Are you ready to get started? Please go to Chapter 1 and let your parents read their introduction.

Introduction For Parents

Thank you for finding *You Can't Bully Me* and sharing it with your child. I know there are dozens of books about what bullying is, why it occurs and what to do about it. This book is different in that your child will work towards self-awareness and confidence without revenge in mind towards the bully or him/herself. Him and her, and he and she will be used interchangeably throughout.

I was bullied in middle school. Back then, kids were expected to handle the situation on their own and, quite frankly, it was not as bad as it is today. In our society, bullying has escalated to a more insistent and hurtful epidemic. It is not just teasing anymore. It has been said that television shows, movies and videogames have made bullying socially acceptable because the dialogue in these types of media is nasty and people laugh at it. The programs in place in school districts describe what bullying is and why it is wrong to do, but there isn't any help for the victim, until now.

There is an activity your child will do, in the Introduction for Kids, exploring sense of self, based on what is said by others compared to what they think on their own.

Depending on your child's age, some assistance from you will be necessary, mostly with vocabulary, but the written work should be the child's alone. I strongly advocate discussion of the concepts, especially when you and your child can talk about experiences the child has had in addition to the stories I tell as introduction to each activity.

Please respect your child's point of view. Your child sees things through a child's eyes. Processing life in a healthy way is one of the goals here. Having said this, you will be able to monitor progress through conversation. Don't rush through; some ideas may need a few days of thought and conversation before your child can make sense of the concept in order to write anything about it.

Your child is in a fragile state. Most thoughts are about school, the bully and the terrible feelings connected to it. If you can, take your child on more outings and/or spend some money on supplies for a new hobby. Sitting around having a pity party is the cycle I want to break; we need to give the kids something else to occupy their attention.

As adults, we have an auto-filter that helps us dismiss or act on the things around us in an appropriate way. The anecdotes and activities presented here are designed to switch the focus from what is happening outside to what is happening inside, addressing your child's belief system about himself. The bully may not stop the bullying, but your child can stop feeling bad about it. Your child is learning, in a very obvious way, what friendship should not be.

My goal and strategy are simple: I think a confident child will not be the victim of a bully. When approached, a confident child will be able to make light of any words a bully might use. I can't speak to violence against a child, though confidence will help with bravery.

I don't have all the answers and I'm not presenting many facts about bullying. There are plenty of resources online, at the library and at bookstores. Part of the formula is matching a possible solution to your particular situation.

Take a few minutes to discuss the activities I asked your child to do in the Introduction For Kids. It's a good place to get started.

Chapter 1

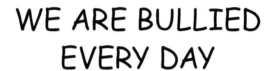

WE ARE BULLIED
EVERY DAY

No one is in charge of your happiness except you.

The people in your life who present you with the greatest challenges are often your best teachers.

You can't control things, but you can control your reaction to things.

Bullying is an every day occurrence, even towards grown-ups. Think about it:

- being cut off in traffic,
- when someone honks the horn to make the driver go faster,
- the neighbor who tells you to cut your grass,
- when someone makes fun of how you behave....you get the idea.

Every time someone insists you do things their way, you are experiencing a form of bullying. Some of the things on this list don't seem like such a big deal to you, do they?

How you react or respond is an indication of your emotional connection to it. None of the things listed deserve any energy or worry.

Activity: List some places outside of school where you think bullying happens. They don't have to be things that have happened to you; perhaps you have noticed something happening to someone else and you didn't like what you saw. Next to the occurrence, write how it made you feel inside and how it made you feel about the person it was happening to.

_____

_____

_____

_____

_____

_____

_____

_____

_____

_____

_____

_____

_____

_____

_____

_____

_____

_____

_____

_____

Note: The bully is teaching you that they don't have what it takes to be your friend. Let me say this again:

the bully does not have what it takes to be your friend.

You choose who your friends are.
You choose how you spend your time together.
This is part of your power; keep it and use it.

Chapter 2

WHO IS THE BULLY?

You're probably thinking the best answers to this question would be: someone at school, someone at afterschool care, your brother or sister. It's possible. But I am focusing on the one you meet in school.

Nevertheless, I think that every time you make a mistake, even a little one, and in your head, you call yourself bad names, then the bully is you. The old-fashioned expression is You Are Your Own Worst Enemy.

What do you tell yourself when you mess up?

_____

_____

_____

_____

_____

_____

_____

_____

I'm guessing that you tell yourself a combination of pep talks and hurtful thoughts too.

Which one might make you feel better: telling yourself "You're such a dummy!" or "What a dumb thing to do." Do you think you're dumb about everything? I don't think so. One comment is directed at you in your heart. The other talks only about the thing that happened. What words would you say to your friend whose feelings are hurt?

_____

_____

_____

_____

_____

_____

_____

_____

_____

Why don't you say them to yourself? Do you think you deserve being bullied? No, no, no, you do not.

People talk and write books about forgiveness all the time. It's a difficult thing to do, forgiving yourself. Pick one thing that doesn't go well for you and start the process of forgiving yourself. How? Apologize to yourself for something.

_____

_____

_____

_____

_____

_____

_____

_____

_____

_____

_____

_____

_____

_____

_____

_____

For me, it's about my weight. My weight is completely my own fault. I don't look the way I would really like to look. Some days, it's easy to watch what I eat, and some days it's not. It's a long process – it took a long time to get to be this size, and it will take a long time to get back down to a reasonable and healthy size. Every day is a chance to start over and do better.

Everyone wants to be perfect all the time, and they are afraid of what might happen if they aren't. Does this describe you? The not-so-secret secret is that it's impossible.

Goal: be the best you can be at this moment in time.

Be a hero for yourself.

Chapter 3

WHAT DO YOU THINK IS WRONG ABOUT YOU? WHAT ARE THE THINGS YOU CAN'T CHANGE?

There is a lot of work in this chapter. Please don't do all the work in one day; I truly want you to think about your feelings.

Let go of what was, accept what is, and have faith in what will be. Past, present and future.

Activity: honestly write what you think is 'wrong' about you.

_____

_____

_____

_____

_____

_____

_____

_____

_____

_____

Notice that I did not give you a lot of space in which to write. What sort of hateful things did you write? Did you write the things the bully is saying to you? Would you ever say those things to someone else to hurt them? Why do you say them to yourself?

There are so many things you can't change....

Height story: Shawn was the shortest boy in fifth grade, and was quick-witted and serious about school. He was also an excellent basketball player. The boys figured out how to get to him – they teased him about his height and this teasing caused him to fistfight. One day, while Shawn was in tears, storming off the court, I was able to get him to walk and talk with me. I made the point that there was nothing he could do about his height and that in fact he should be celebrating it because he was fast on his feet and could easily get under the taller boys to steal the ball, which he did all the time. That made him laugh, and he admitted that he was proud of himself for being able to do that.

This-is-how-I-was-born story: Another young man I admire is now a motivational speaker and travels the world to share his story. His name is Nick Vujicic. Nick was born without arms and legs (he has a partial foot on one side). He was teased in school so much, he thought about killing himself because he didn't see how he could ever be happy and live any kind of normal life. He changed his mind because his family had been really loving and supportive and he didn't want to hurt them by doing it. Instead, Nick tried to do everything everybody else did (sometimes with success but sometimes not), and learned how to do many things. Watch the video that introduced him to me: http://www.cbsnews.com/videos/against-all-odds/. He is thankful for everything he does have instead of being angry for everything he doesn't have.

Check in: How do you feel about the stories you just read?

_____

_____

_____

_____

_____

_____

_____

Money story: I don't believe in buying things you can't afford. If you're being bulled (or if you're bullying yourself) because you can't afford to get a new toy, then we have a bigger issue to discuss. You must be grateful for what you do have. If you want something else, then step up your game. If you get an allowance, save more of your money. I promise you, everything you buy for yourself will mean more to you because you earned it.

Another side of this would be, why do you want the latest toy? If you really don't need it for your life and you want it because everyone else is getting one, then you have to learn gratitude. I owned my last car for 22 years. I took very good care of it; not having a car payment allowed me to go on vacation and have other things in my life; teachers don't make a lot of money. My budget isn't big enough to keep replacing things that aren't broken. The television in my bedroom is 25 years old. I only watch TV in the bedroom when I lay down to go to sleep; why spend money on a flat screen when I don't really need it? Do you understand my point?

Gratitude Journal: Every day may not be good, but there is something good in every day.

Every day, you will be writing at least three things that you were grateful for that day. You can write in any kind of book you like. I use a small 3"x5" spiral notebook and my three usually fit on one sheet.

For example, mine for today are:

1. I got home with groceries before the thunderstorm,
2. It only took a couple of minutes to find the math mistake in my checkbook (I had reversed two numbers), and
3. A friend called and asked me to go out to dinner.

None of these seems extraordinary, but each of them made me smile. That's all it takes.

Gratitude Story: Patti was the oldest of four kids. She was always taking care of her younger siblings and complaining about it. One Monday, I overheard her crying to her best friend about how she had gone to a picnic the day before and no one paid attention to her. When I found out the source of her upset, I pointed out that she had been given the day off from caretaking. I asked her if she had alone time to draw and read (she had), and whether her mother found her when it was time to eat (she did). This poor girl didn't enjoy a perfectly lovely day outdoors because she didn't realize what she had. She was too busy focusing on something she didn't have (and thought she wanted) and missed out on gratitude.

Write your first gratitude journal entry with today's date:

_____

_____

_____

_____

_____

_____

_____

_____

_____

_____

_____

Check In: Do these stories make sense to you? Do you think you can switch your thinking around and be glad for your stuff instead of sad?

_____

_____

_____

_____

_____

_____

_____

_____

_____

_____

_____

_____

———————————————————————

———————————————————————

———————————————————————

———————————————————————

———————————————————————

———————————————————————

———————————————————————

———————————————————————

———————————————————————

———————————————————————

Other things you can't change include your skin color, the shape of your face, the history of your family, your culture.

You are unique.

You are best at being you, whoever that may be.

You are perfect at being imperfect.

Chapter 4

WHAT DO YOU THINK IS RIGHT ABOUT YOU? WHAT ARE THE THINGS YOU CAN CHANGE?

There is a lot of work in this chapter too. Again, please don't do all the work in one day; I truly want you to think about your feelings.

Be someone who makes you happy instead of being with someone who makes you happy.

Activity: what's 'right' about you? Use highlighters, and colored pencils to circle or underline all the compliments you write to yourself.

_____

_____

_____

_____

_____

_____

_____

_____

_____

Did you include: clever, kind, mischievous, funny, creative, strong, friendly, smart, leader, neat, curious, loveable, silly, optimistic, brave, generous, determined, good-looking, angelic, cool, athletic, clean, gentle, organized, thoughtful, brilliant, nature lover, inquisitive, daring, hopeful, adventurous, caring, persevering, honest, special, happy, big-hearted, fashionable, inventive, joyful, powerful, loving, cuddly, polite, forgiving, artistic, graceful, powerful, inspirational, sensitive, joyous, charming, peaceful? If any of these is missing from your list and you like it, add it now and highlight it. The choices are limitless. Be who you want to be!

On which list should we put scared, unsure, lonely, careful? Actually, these are normal things and belong on both lists. It's healthy to feel these things. Crying is healthy, too, for girls and boys.

Check In: How do you feel about yourself now?

_____

_____

_____

_____

How do you feel about the bully?

_____

_____

_____

_____

_____

_____

_____

_____

_____

_____

_____

_____

_____

_____

_____

_____

_____

_____

_____

_____

_____

_____

_____

Love yourself like your life depends on it, because it does.

The past is over. It can't hurt you any more.

Compassion – Have it for everyone, especially yourself. Hug yourself every day. Give yourself credit for everything that went well during the day, and make an action plan for the things that didn't turn out well. Most of all, applaud your efforts and forgive your shortcomings. Practice and you will improve.

Every book you read about bullying will tell you that it's not you, it's the bully. The bully is angry, and doesn't have self-esteem or confidence.

We aren't focusing on changing that person. We aren't focusing on changing you. Keep liking all the things you like. Keep being nerdy, geeky, weird, and funny, if those are the words you call yourself (these words describe me), and celebrate yourself. Like yourself for being the way you are. Keep going!

Things I don't like: licorice, root beer, peppermint, spicy foods, fart jokes, plaid, vampire and monster movies, roller coasters. Should I apologize for not liking this stuff? I just don't like them. Just because I'm not a good cook, does it mean I can't eat? You do what you can, when you can.

Look how many choices there are in the world. Despite all the color choices in the paint store, people still combine colors to create something new. Same thing goes with music. The same notes and chords are available for every musician to use. Look how many songs there are! Words – look how many books there are about so many different things! Cars, clothes, sneakers, and so forth.

When you visit someone in their home, does it look like your house? Does everyone drive the same car? Would you want someone else's bedroom to look like yours? Think about it. These are examples of things you want to be different; why are you so busy worrying that you might not be the same as everyone else?

There are things you <u>can</u> change:

Hygiene: You must bathe every day and use deodorant if necessary. You must wear clean clothes, or at least clean underwear and socks, and a clean shirt when you can. I also have a thing about hands, so trim your nails and wash the dirt out from under them. If you think you look good, you will feel good too.

Check In: What can you do to take better care of yourself?

_____

_____

_____

_____

_____

Smarts: Well, as a teacher, you just know I will tell you to do your homework. Also, read, read, read, anything and everything. Practicing school will give you better grades and expand your knowledge. Knowledge is power. On my board every year, I wrote this rhyme: The more you learn, the more you earn. It's true.

Check In: Which school subject do you need to work harder to master? They are all connected; how can you start doing your best?

_____

_____

_____

_____

_____

_____

_____

_____

_____

Athletic ability: Are you on a team? How many practices are you allowed to miss before you're kicked off the team? Practicing your particular skill and working it with a team is what practice is all about. The expression is "Everyone brings something to the party." One person can't play all the positions. Learn about sportsmanship and fair play because you'll be living these for the rest of your life.

If you're not on a team, you still need to work your body. Look around at all the older people with walkers and canes. I'm not suggesting you take up a sport and train for the Olympics; just do some activities you like every day to keep your body strong and healthy. I don't care how much you weigh; I care that you will be able to keep moving and enjoy your life.

Check In: Make a list of activities you really like so you can choose one to do every day:

_____

_____

_____

_____

Weight story: Let me tell you about Tim. Tim is a voracious (look it up; it's a great word) reader. Instead of playing at recess, he always chose to read. Reading was his escape. I found out he was being bullied by the kid in class who was bullying everyone who wasn't in his group and/or wasn't athletic. I called Tim into the classroom one morning before the bell rang to find out what was going on and where it was happening. He told me the boy had been calling him fat names and wouldn't stop despite being asked.

I thought about it for a minute and then asked him what his reaction would be to being called stupid. Tim looked at me with a puzzled expression and asked me if I was serious. I nodded. Tim said that was ridiculous. Okay, I said, why? Tim said he knew he is smart. So, I said, maybe when this other boy is calling you fat, it bothers you because there's some truth to it? Tim blushed and I could see I had embarrassed him a little. I asked Tim if someone commented that I had gained a few pounds and I patted my belly and agreed, would that person say anything to me about it again? He said probably not. So, Tim, I continued, you have two choices. You can pat your belly and smile or you can do something about it. By the time, three weeks later, we had returned from spring break, Tim had lost five pounds and admitted that he felt better. The bully couldn't call him fat anymore.

Check In: Did I offer Tim a reasonable solution? Why or why not?

_____

_____

_____

_____

_____

_____

_____

_____

_____

_____

_____

_____

_____

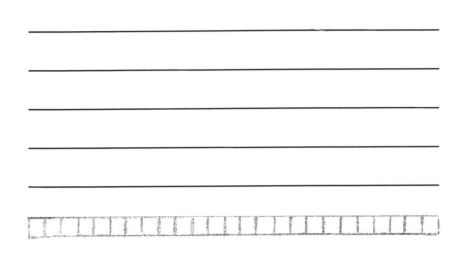

Culture: Everyone in this country came from somewhere else. Trace your history to the first person in your family who came to America. Chances are you will find out that life was very difficult in the beginning. The thing that people relied on most was the way of life they had before. Customs and traditions are very important to most people. I enjoy lighting Hanukkah candles with my Jewish friends as much as decorating a Christmas tree with my Catholic friends. I like the idea of dance as prayer, which is part of almost every culture.

My advice is to embrace where your family came from and enjoy your history. It is part of what makes you special and different; these are good differences. Anyone who teases you is trying to embarrass you about yourself.

Check In: Do you feel proud of your family? Why do you allow anyone to challenge your love?

_____

_____

_____

_____

_____

_____

_____

_____

_____

_____

_____

_____

_____

_____

_____

_____

_____

_____

_____

_____

_____

_____

_____

_____

The bully will throw out a bunch of statements and keep coming back to the one that makes you react because that's what makes you the target. This is called "pushing your buttons." The bully is really, really good at pushing them. Does the bully ever say mean things to other kids when the friends aren't around? Probably not. The bully loses power when no one is around.

Activity: Please read the stories again, and list which 'wrong' things you think you can take off the list right now and how your opinion has changed.

_____

_____

_____

_____

_____

_____

_____

_____

_____

_____

_____

_____

_____

_____

_____

_____

_____

_____

_____

_____

_____

_____

_____

_____

_____

_____

_____

Chapter 5

WHAT ARE YOU
AFRAID OF?

Have your fears, but don't become your fears.

The hardest thing in the world to do is to be true to yourself. Along with that comes the realization that you won't be able to please everyone. The secret of this is that you should never waste your time trying.

If you stop yourself from doing things because you are afraid of what someone else says, pretty soon, you stop being yourself. When you do that, you end up feeling disappointed in yourself without understanding why.

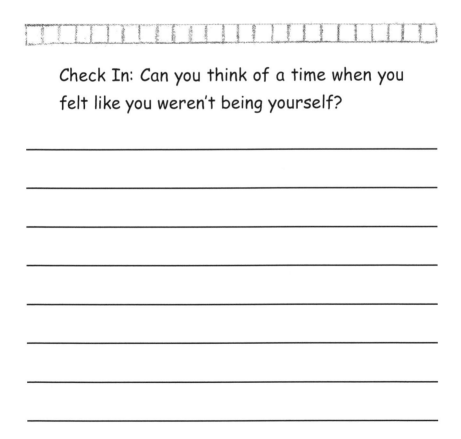

Check In: Can you think of a time when you felt like you weren't being yourself?

_____

_____

_____

_____

_____

_____

_____

Check In: When you are upset, what do you do?

_____

_____

_____

_____

_____

_____

_____

_____

_____

_____

_____

_____

_____

_____

_____

_____

_____

_____

_____

Do you tell yourself more bad things or do you try to give yourself a pep talk? Do you eat too much, or play games instead of taking care of your responsibilities (chores, homework, etc)? When one thing goes wrong, it doesn't mean that everything is wrong or should be wrong. Separate that one thing so that you can work a little harder on it until it improves.

Do you know the story of Snow White and The Seven Dwarves? Each of them has different names. Do you realize that their names are specific to their personalities? Sneezy is the one that sneezes all the time. Bashful is the shy dwarf. Doc is the smartest one, right, because we all assume a doctor would be smart. The only reason they think Dopey is a dope is because he does not talk, but he's smarter than he seems. And Grumpy is, well, grumpy, and always in a bad mood. But his bad mood is the one who watches out for everyone else the best. The group of them contributes their collected talents to make life good for the rest. And they need each other.

Check In: Who do you need? Who needs you? How?

_____

_____

_____

_____

_____

_____

_____

_____

_____

_____

Chapter 6

CONFIDENCE

I saw a picture in a restroom once that shows a kitten looking into a mirror and a lion is staring back at him. The kitten knows what it will become. Do you?

Activity: What's your best thing? What are you really good at doing?

_____

_____

_____

_____

_____

_____

How do you know?

_____

_____

_____

_____

_____

What other things are you good at?

_____

_____

_____

_____

_____

_____

_____

_____

_____

_____

_____

_____

_____

Check In: How does it feel to write these things and look at them? I hope you feel proud.

_____

_____

_____

_____

_____

_____

_____

_____

_____

_____

_____

_____

_____

Check In: What I would like you to do is think first and then write about why you have the confidence in these things. Were you so interested in something that you learned more about it and practiced? Did you do something because friends or siblings did it?

_____

_____

_____

_____

_____

_____

_____

_____

_____

_____

_____

_____

_____

_____

_____

_____

_____

_____

What exactly is confidence? It's a feeling that you can do something, yes, but it is also when you know that you know something. When you put in time and effort and become an expert at something, your confidence about that thing is huge. And, I'll tell you, when you feel it for the first time, you want to use that same energy to feel it again about something else. So, you put your time and effort into something new.

You need to be your own something new so you can find your confidence. It's somewhere inside you; you just have to trust yourself. Will you mess up sometimes? Absolutely! But, your feelings about yourself when you mess up will make all the difference in gaining your confidence.

The big word for when you keep on trying is resilience. Resilience is the really good quality of continuing to try when you don't think you can. I think the bully sees that you aren't very confident about yourself.

I want you to take this confidence and apply it to other things in your life where you don't feel as confident. Is it lack of effort? Is it lack of skill? Is it lack of knowledge? Is it lack of resources or supplies? Is it lack of a partner or team? In the end, no matter the reason, you need to make peace with what you are able to do right now.

Let's change that by starting with something easy. At which game are you the best? Do you win 100% of the time? Probably not. When your score isn't as high as 'usual,' don't you just start over? Absolutely! But, if you pound the keyboard or screen while you play, are you having fun? No. Are you improving? No.

In school, when do you raise your hand? When you do know, or when you don't know? Hopefully, you have a teacher who takes your wrong answer and guides you to the right one. And, don't you feel victorious? Don't you (suddenly) feel brilliant? You knew the answer was there and your teacher helped you find it.

I don't bowl a game that's over 100 points. But, guess what? I still go bowling. I can't sing well, so I sing in my car. I'm also not good at drawing, dancing, or sports. You get the idea? I not only accept this about myself, sometimes I joke about it too. I have other interests I like that don't require mastery, like reading, watching movies, riding my bike and taking a walk.

In every game or contest, there is a winner and a loser.

Poem

You can't bully me, of this I am proud
You can't bully me, I'll say it aloud
Your words, taunts and laughter don't get to me at all
I know who I am, and how to stand tall.

Chapter 7

WHAT CAN YOU DO TO HONOR YOURSELF?

Do you make a New Year's resolution every year? Why not choose to love yourself more?

People will come and go during the course of your life, but the person in the mirror will always be with you, so be good to yourself.

During the series of anti-bullying lessons in school, I used to ask my class to brainstorm things they could do when they are hurting and need to feel better.

So, that's your task here. On the next page, I'll make some suggestions.

_____

_____

_____

_____

_____

_____

_____

_____

_____

_____

_____

_____

_____

_____

_____

_____

_____

_____

_____

_____

_____

_____

When you need to feel better, you can:

1 - Cry it out – your body will calm down and you'll be able to think clearly

2 - Have a (healthy) snack

3 - Clean your room - the activity distracts you and keeps you moving – or rearrange the furniture so it looks new

4 - Listen to music – no sad songs allowed

5 - Do a really good job on your homework and study

6 - Take a walk or ride your bike – but not on the street where the bully lives

7 - Read – going inside a good story provides a mini-vacation from your thoughts

8 - Watch a movie that makes you laugh

9 - Do yoga or another quiet physical activity that requires concentration

10 - Talk things out with someone you completely trust – saying it aloud helps too

11 - Draw

12 - Write in a journal

13 - Make goofy faces at yourself in the mirror to make yourself laugh

14 - Take a bath and play in the bubbles

15 - Dance

16 - Play a game

17 - Meditate (books from the library or videos online)
18 - Work on your hobby – if you don't have one, start one
19 - Fly a kite
20 - Pray – for people you care about, including yourself
21 - Count to ten – for fun, learn how to count in another language
22 - Lay down in the grass and watch the clouds in the sky
23 - Take a book or video from the library and learn something new (I'm learning Tai Chi.)

This list was created by my whole class. Usually each student was able to think of five or six, but when you put them all together, look how many choices there are!

Chapter 8

INTENTIONS

If you think you can, you can. If you think you can't, you can't. Both are right.

Depending on the grade you're in, you probably know all about the Author's Purpose in reading and writing. For primary grades, the first letters of the words for author's purpose spell the word pie: persuade, inform, entertain.

I have always taught persuade by using the connection to television commercials. What is the purpose of the commercial? To persuade you to buy a product. The intention when the commercial is created might include information about the product and entertainment because people like to buy products when they like the commercials. So, while all three elements might be present, the persuasive intention is the most important one in commercials. In fact, Super Bowl commercials have become so famous, many people watch the game just for the entertainment of the commercials.

When advertisers make their commercials and even magazine/newspaper ads, you are their target. Their intention is to make you want to do only one thing: spend your money on their stuff. There is nothing hurtful or evil in what they do.

Let's talk about the bully. What is the bully's intention in bullying you? Make a list of the ideas that have been running through your head.

_____

_____

_____

_____

_____

_____

_____

_____

_____

_____

_____

_____

_____

_____

I think the bully's intention is to feel superior over someone. Feeling superior means that they think they are better than you are. To look powerful to his friends. To feel tough. To look fearless. To make someone unhappy. Just to be mean. Notice, please, that I didn't say anything about you. This isn't about you, as I tried to explain before. You just happen to be available.

Let's talk about your intention. I completely understand if you feel angry. I also understand if you want revenge. Sadly, you are not the person who can do anything about it. You can not hurt someone who doesn't care about you. Let me repeat this: you can not hurt someone who doesn't care about you.

Your intention needs to be about you and about becoming a better, stronger version of yourself. There is no competition; however, there is a prize. The prize will be a happier life.

Chapter 9

FRIENDSHIP

Name the person with whom you feel the most comfortable. Now, can you write about how you feel when you're with that person?

_____

_____

_____

_____

_____

_____

_____

_____

_____

_____

_____

_____

_____

_____

_____

_____

_____

_____

_____

For me, the most comfortable feeling with my friends is not doing anything special, talking about things that matter and things that don't, and just hanging out together. I know that I am accepted, and appreciated.

I know that my friends value my opinion, especially when we don't agree. I feel calm, happy, safe, and relaxed.

When you're with someone who makes you nervous and you worry about saying or doing the wrong thing, it's your body telling you to watch out and be careful.

Which feeling is more natural? Find the people you can be comfortable with.

Your friends want the best for you. They will tell you the truth, especially when they think you might be doing something that could hurt you. And, they don't want anything back from you except the same thing.

Friends are the people you want to spend your time with, being silly, and having fun.

Check In: What does friendship mean to you?

_____

_____

_____

_____

_____

_____

_____

_____

_____

_____

_____

_____

_____

_____

_____

_____

_____

_____

_____

_____

_____

_____

_____

_____

_____

_____

_____

Chapter 10

WHO ARE YOU
BETTER THAN?

Can you answer this question honestly? You are better than no one. You might be a better cook, dancer, tennis player, runner, whatever, than someone else, but that doesn't make you better than anyone. It only makes you better at something compared to someone else. And I'll tell you, there's somebody out there who is better at these things than you are.

How do you feel about this? You can be better every day. When you learn more about friendship, your behavior tells how much better you are. When you show kindness and compassion to others, you are behaving in a better way. Start with yourself. Treat yourself kindly, with gentleness and love.

The goal here is to get you to think about how you live your life, and accept your decisions with your whole heart. When you do that, no one can bully you about it.

Chapter 11

MEDITATION

Everything we have discussed is related to emotions. Your feelings are being hurt. I think you will find a way to ignore the bully, but it's going to take some work.

Meditation is the practice of sitting quietly to silence the mind and stop thinking your thoughts for a while. What this does is take your focus away from your problems and let you calm down.

You won't need more than one minute to start, and, in the beginning, one minute is a long time. Do as much as you can. Add more time when you find that you like how this feels.

When you close your eyes, picture all the things that bother you. No matter what your inner vision is, don't let emotions enter your body; just look at your thoughts, say hello to them, and let them pass. I see them written on clouds that I can gently push like balloons that are losing air and they float away. My friend sees her thoughts on a white board that she erases. Maybe they're written on billboards and they move past you like they would in a moving car.

You can also try saying a mantra. A mantra is a sentence you repeat for the whole time you are meditating. By focusing on those words, you can't focus on your thoughts. Start with "Peace begins with me," and as you say it, press your thumb against each of your fingers as if you were counting the words.

Sometimes, when I can't push the thoughts aside, I listen to music sung in a foreign language so I can't understand the words and the music calms me. Whichever way you try is correct for you.

Afterwards, you will feel calmer, more relaxed and more in control of your feelings.

This is the best way to clear your head.

Check In: Which way to meditate is the best for you? (Of course, you had to have tried them all.)

_____

_____

_____

_____

_____

Chapter 12

AFTERWARDS

You can only be yourself. You can be someone else only if you are acting. So many people are afraid of who they are, that they pretend every day. I think that's sad.

The only person who needs to accept you is you. You have to accept all those things that you are not and think you should be. Your talents will show themselves if you pay attention to the activities you like to do the most.

Did you see the show Kids Cook-off this summer? There was a competition between two teams of four kids each and Rachael and Guy, two of the most popular chefs on television, coached them.

You might wonder why I would watch a cooking show that starred kids instead of grown ups. Simple; each of those kids can cook better than me. I thought I would learn something from them. Obviously, then, I am not a good cook. I should wear a sign. Yeah, I make stuff to eat, but what I do can't be called cooking, at least not like that. :D

But seriously, it's going to take a little while before you figure things out. But one day, as soon as that same person says something mean to you, you won't care.

In *You Can't Bully Me*, you learned about yourself and your values, and you learned to accept who you are. By putting your thoughts on paper, you discovered the things that are important to you. Please, don't give up on those things. Those things are the path to your happiness. They have your interest and your passion. Go after them and shine! Shine for yourself and no one else.

Time heals all wounds, just give it some time.

So, now that you feel better, what are you going to do? When you see bullying happen, you have firsthand knowledge of how much it hurts. Reach out to other kids and form your own group – not for bullying, of course - to help each other build confidence and explore your interests. You'll make real friends, and feel really good about yourself.

You can't bully me about the music I like, the food I like to eat, the kinds of movies I prefer (nothing scary, thank you very much). Get the idea?

You are important and you matter. Your feelings matter. Your voice matters. Your story matters. Your life matters.....Always.

Everything is better when you're happy. When you're not, remember that happiness is just around the corner, waiting for you to get there.

Once a week, I'd like you to take out this book and leaf through it to reread all the compliments you wrote to yourself and put in color. A year from now, read the whole book from the beginning and marvel at how much you've grown and changed.

Promise me you'll always remember:

You're braver than you believe, and stronger than you seem, and smarter than you think.

– Winnie The Pooh

NOTES

NOTES

NOTES

NOTES

NOTES

NOTES

NOTES

NOTES

NOTES

NOTES

NOTES